# THE SECRET OF
# ST. MARGARET MARY

SAINT MARGARET MARY
(*Maurice Denis*)

# THE SECRET OF
# ST. MARGARET MARY

*by*

HENRI GHEON

*Translated by*

F. J. SHEED

NEW YORK
SHEED & WARD
1937

NIHIL OBSTAT: REGINALDUS PHILLIPS, S.TH.L.

CENSOR DEPUTATUS

IMPRIMATUR: L. CAN. EVANS,

VIC. GEN.

WESTMONASTERII, DII 17A MARTII 1937

# THE SECRET OF
## ST. MARGARET MARY

I

THE twenty-seventh of December is the feast of St. John the Evangelist, who rested his head on the Saviour's breast. On that day in the year 1673, to a humble sister at prayer the same grace was given. And when she raised her head again, her Master laid upon her this burden of His love: 'My divine Heart is so wrought with love for men and in especial for you, that it can no longer contain the flame of the fire of its love but must spread this flame through you and manifest itself to men to enrich them with its precious treasures: these I show you: they contain the sanctifying and saving graces needed to draw men back from the pit of perdition. And for the accomplishment of this great design, I have chosen you as an abyss of unworthiness and ignorance, *in order that all should be wrought by me.*' 'Thereupon,' she continues, 'he asked me for my heart which I prayed him to take; which he did, and placed it in his own adorable heart wherein he showed it to me *like a tiny atom being consumed in that blazing furnace*; and he drew it forth again like a burning flame in the form of a heart, and set it once more in the place whence he had taken it . . .'

'Like a tiny atom . . .' That image says all, fixing thus simply and precisely her rôle and her personality in the eyes of her Master and in the eyes of men. The sheer immensity of St. Margaret Mary's mission — to revive, exalt, consecrate anew in the Church of God the devotion to Christ's love — has ensured the eclipse of her self. As she desired, so it has been: in the universal chorus of praise and prayer aroused by her, she herself is either forgotten, or more often seen but not regarded. The figure of a heart surmounted by a cross is in our homes and on our banners. Upon her who put it there, our minds do not linger. Her memory is no more to us than a point of fire lost in the great flame.

II

Had it been left to her, we should have known nothing about her, nothing whatsoever. Her superiors commanded her to speak and with death in her soul, she obeyed. It was necessary that she speak, to establish the new devotion, and still more to justify it; for it was an offence alike to Protestant and Jansenist and Rationalist, to all the varieties of human error which set a limit to God's right of loving men or his power of loving men or the means He may use to win men's love. It was necessary that she speak — as every day brings proof — to prevent the new devotion from degenerating into fetichism and mere superstition, to save it from the pretty-pretty insipidity to which the pious can reduce all devotions whatsoever not sparing even that, the keenest-edged, which glorifies the Sacred Fire of Love which the

Son of God came to cast upon the earth that it might be enkindled.

What is that Heart we are called upon to worship? What is the worship we are called upon to pay it? St. Margaret Mary tells us. Yet she is not the first to tell us. From St. John onwards Christians have venerated the Sacred Heart. St. John in a vision brought St. Gertrude within its presence. Laid open on the cross, it sent forth a ray to wound the heart of the Little Poor Man of Assisi. St. Catherine of Siena, receiving it in exchange for her own, felt it beating in her breast. And there are more. Nor should we forget that almost contemporary with our Saint is Marie des Vallées, a penitent of St. John Eudes, who saw the Sacred Heart, knew it for what it was, and loved it. But clearly it was God's plan to reserve to the humble Visitandine nun of Paray-le-Monial the decisive rôle in the propagation of that mysterious flame. From earliest childhood, she lived in the intimacy of the Heart of Jesus.

No saint has ever known or loved it better; and we learn the price she had to pay as we read the note-book which she meant for her superiors only, which on her death-bed she implored them to destroy.

To pay homage to the Heart of Jesus means quite simply to accept the Cross, to seek out the Cross, to die to the world upon the Cross. And all this one can do only through love — and through love of Love Itself. In her day Love was no longer loved. It was a dry hard faith that they preached. So God showed men His Heart. They were deaf to the lesson of St. John at the Last Supper, to the lesson of St. Gertrude and the singer of Assisi and the tertiary of Siena, to the plain lesson of the Gospel itself. Very well then. If the blind crowd needed a sign that even the blind could not miss: a blazing, bleeding, burning sign of the uncompre-hended Love which bleeds and burns for all: a poor girl who had surrendered herself wholly should receive the clue to the secret, the sign, and should deliver it to men in her own immolation.

III

MARGARET MARY ALACOQUE — what a god-send that ludicrous surname for the Voltaires and their kind—was the daughter of a royal notary who lived at Lautecour, a small village in the diocese of Autun. The Charolais is a pleasant region, level enough but not too level, a place of willows and grass-lands; wide stretches of grey-green that are almost almond, oxen and cows white all over, and a sky that can be as white as the cattle. If its quiet charm had any attraction for Margaret Mary, she turned away, not yielding to it. She is not of the number of the Converted, whom God leaves to be worked upon by nature to the point where His grace may overcome them and make its own of them on some Damascus road. She is of the number of the Preserved, in whom He dwells with power from the beginning and upon whom He traces, as on a blank page, the exactions of His will.

She was born on July 22nd in the year 1647; just before the troubles of the Fronde, a little longer before Louis XIV was to commence that mighty reign which looks so meagre beside the kingdom that her Master would use her to establish over the whole earth. Fittingly enough it was on the feast of St. Mary Magdalen that she began her life, the life which was to be all prayer and penance — the sins of a whole age to bear, all that was wanting in man's love for God to be made up in her. All the realm of Heaven was astir: the multitude of angels and saints were at her birth, and the Blessed Virgin, and Jesus. But if Heaven was with her, earth was less friendly. Upon earth she found little aid but rebuffs in plenty, in the world and in the cloister, from the good as from the wicked, from her natural family as from her religious. All her life she was to be a kind of no-man's-land endlessly fought over by two armies interlocked, the army of earth and the army of heaven. We shall understand nothing of her marvellous adventure unless we take our stand at that mysterious point where nature and super-nature stand face to face and at issue; our poor psychologies can make no sense of it at all.

The fifth child, she was placed almost at once in the home of her godmother, Mme de Fautrières, mistress of the Château of Corcheval. Her god-mother gave her into the care of two servants — one, of evil life, was all honey to the child, who found her repulsive; the other, of bleak virtue, treated her harshly; but this one the child pre-ferred. Even so young, she could *smell* sin; she scented it. She did not know what chastity was — she was three! — but she made a vow of chastity to God. 'To check me in all the boisterousness of childhood, they had but to tell me that a thing would offend God; that checked me instantly and

15

drew me back from what I had been minded to do.'

Yet she loved play; and would give it up to go —
often enough — to a little oak wood and there pray
kneeling on the ground, her knees bare. It is common enough of course for children to perform odd
feats, of piety or anything else, to catch the attention
of grown-ups; Margaret Mary's one fear was that
anyone should come upon her thus in prayer.

Her father died suddenly; her mother could not
be bothered with her. She was sent to board with
the Urbanist nuns at Charolles. At nine, she made
her first Communion. 'This communion,' she
wrote, 'made all the small pleasures and amuse-
ments so repellent to me, that I could no longer
take pleasure in any . . . just when I wanted to
begin some game with my companions, I would
always feel *something* drawing me, calling me to
some quiet corner, giving me no peace till I had
followed and then setting me to pray.' It was no
longer herself in action — it was *something*, or
someone, acting in her and for her. Such a relation

with God, so early entered into, was a sure sign of vocation. As was fitting, proofs of vocation followed quickly.

For four years she was ill, unable to stir a limb; her bones 'pierced her skin all over'. All remedies failing, she was dedicated to the Blessed Virgin; the child promised that one day she would be 'one of her daughters' and in that instant she was cured. Was the bias towards self that is in every human nature since Adam's sin thereby made straight in her? It was not. Her one thought was the pleasure she might take in the enjoyment of her recovered liberty. God sent her persecution.

Upon her father's death, a relation — one Toussaint Delaroche — had claimed authority over the house in the interests of the family property. All power was taken from the widow, who was weak and helpless by nature; and, so writes the saint: 'Certain others prevailed in such wise that never were we, she and I, in such captivity. It was a continual warfare; everything was kept under lock and key, so that often I could not even find anything to wear to Mass and must borrow clothes and bonnet.' Then she would hide in a corner of the garden or the cowshed, remaining there for days at a time without food or drink; the moment she reappeared 'the warfare began again worse than before'. In one of these nights spent in tears at the feet of the Crucified, she learnt that it was God's design to render her in all things 'conformed to His life of suffering'; and all her troubles became light beside her desire 'to suffer still more in order to be conformed to Jesus'.

Even this was but the prelude. Her mother even turned against her. Several eligible men sought her hand; her mother pressed her to marry. 'She wept unceasingly, saying that she had no hope but in me to escape from her suffering in the consolation she would find in coming to be with me when I should have a home in the world.' Margaret Mary loved her mother and let herself be won over little by little. But her vow stood in the way. She invented specious reasons against keeping it: she would not now be strong enough in the convent for the fasts and the scourgings she would desire; the convent demanded a sanctity beyond her powers, and in the failure she would lose her soul. But her vow held her 'as though bound and drawn by cords'. As punishment for her arguments, she bound her body with real cords, with knots sinking into her flesh; her arms she bound round with small chains 'which pulled off flesh when they were removed'. She read the lives of saints; she tells us in all simplicity that she said to herself as she opened the book: 'I must find a saint very easy to imitate, that I may be able to do what she did and become a saint like her.' But God required the maximum from her.

The conflict went on from day to day for nearly three years. Forced to dress well, she chose the quietest materials. Invited out, she made conversation about God and salvation. She practised obedience — to see if she had the character for a nun — in all things save such as ran counter to her vow. She had no one to confide in, no spiritual director, no trace of any human influence. 'Lord, give me someone to guide me!' And God replied: 'Am I not sufficient for thee?'

She was confirmed at twenty-two, and in the strength of the Sacrament she faced her mother's grief, and faced it down. Whereupon pretexts were found for delay — as that her dowry was not ready. She was sent to live with her uncle, Philibert Lamyn, who had a daughter an Ursuline at Mâcon. She promised to arrange for Margaret Mary to enter her convent. 'I do not want you there,' said a mysterious voice. One day she was looking at a portrait of St. Francis de Sales; it seemed to look at her 'with a look so charged with fatherly love' that she realized that he was summoning her. And when she paid a visit to the convent of Paray-le-Monial and entered the parlour, the same mysterious voice spoke again: 'Here is the place.'

IV

W HY the Visitation Order and not, say, the Carmelites? That the contradiction might be maintained. God had cast Margaret Mary into an *extraordinary* way; He would have her tread this way within an order notably prudent, an order which, in the spirit of its Founder, recommends souls to take *ordinary* ways. He set within the four walls of that house a young passionate soul, which had known no direction but His — and which had not the spirit of the house.

What picture of her can we form? Black veil, black robe, her face framed round in white — so much we may know of any Visitation nun; a full face, so it would seem from the rare likeness we have — a family portrait and a statue made later — a face withdrawn and unobserving, or rather looking inwards to where the divine flame was burning. For her outward appearance, let us be satisfied with that. On her arrival in the convent, she asked the mistress of novices how one must pray. 'Place yourself before Our Lord, *like a canvas before the painter.*' What we must find out and hold clear in our minds is the image that Our Lord painted and for twenty years re-touched on that virgin canvas.

Details in plenty can be passed over. The essence of the drama lies in this: Margaret Mary was God's confidante: but Margaret Mary had surrendered her will into the hands of her superiors. On one side, was God's will told her by God; on the other, the obedience due to her superiors and to the Rule. Need there be opposition? Only if God willed it. In the intimate converse of prayer, He constantly required of her certain penances, prescribed certain practices. Obviously, so you might think, she had but to bow before His sovereign Will. But supposing this was not in accord with the will of Mère Hersant, or the novice mistress, or the father-confessor, who were not in the secret? And supposing they should

forbid her to do what God had required of her? . . .
She could but obey them. The Master declared
Himself 'content' that she obeyed the will of her
Superiors and not His will, 'when they forbade her
to do what He had ordered'. A strange conflict,
assuredly, but one that comes frequently in the
story of chosen souls ever since Peter received
upon earth powers that should be ratified in heaven.
God wills no less than His whole will: but He can
will that obstacles should be set in the way of His
will. To accomplish His secret designs, He can
use means which appear to run counter to them.
This time His victory involved a victim, Sister
Margaret Mary, who was to be caught and crushed
as in a vice between His direct power exercised by
Himself and the power He had delegated to men.

The graces she received made her ashamed of
herself. The scepticism and the irony they pro-
voked were in some sense a consolation. Behind
the high close-set grille still to be seen in the chapel,

to the right of the altar, she knelt or lay prostrate; and, in the rays that poured unseen from the Blessed Sacrament enclosed in the tabernacle, she yearned, but in fear and trembling, for the graces which never failed her.

They tried to withdraw her from what she thought was God's voice; they imposed upon her a practical method of prayer with an order of 'points' which she tried hard but in vain to follow; they set her to help the Sister Infirmarian who found not much use in her; they threatened to send her away and postponed her profession. None of it mattered. In all times and places, in all distresses and joys, her Sovereign was her abiding companion. During a retreat she was given charge of an ass and its foal in the garden — 'which', said she, 'did nothing but scamper', and which must be prevented from devouring the plants. She chased after them, her mind on the ass Our Lord rode into Jerusalem, and the palms. Far from being 'impeded' in her prayer, it was during this breathless rushing round that God gave her 'such love for the Cross', that she could 'never more live for a moment without suffering'.

At this period, the most dramatic conflict arose from a sufficiently prosaic object. She had an unconquerable loathing for cheese. Cheese was offered to her in the refectory. She declined it. They insisted. For three days the conflict raged. She wept and moaned before God, begging for the strength to eat it. God made no move to grant her prayer. 'In love, nothing must be held back.' That was the password; she accepted the sacrifice, not once, but again and again; and over a space of twenty years her loathing never lessened. The matter seems to you ludicrous enough; yet her self-conquest won such a redoubling of God's graces and favours that often she cried out: 'O my God, either suspend this torrent that is drowning me in its flood or increase my capacity to receive it.' Suffering, cutting ever deeper, was hollowing a mighty channel for grace.

## V

Mère de saumaise having been made Superior, Margaret Mary was allowed to make her profession. Then God treated her as 'a spouse of Tabor', giving her the joy of His presence in a manner not before experienced by her, the senses playing no part: she could hear Him thus 'much better'. A detailed account of this unbroken converse with God would fill a whole book: but the goal to which all these ecstasies, raptures and mortifications were leading was still unknown to her. Let us pass then to the four solemn manifestations which have to do with the devotion to the Sacred Heart.

The first of these has been related in part at the beginning of this small book. When Our Lord gave her back the heart which He had placed

'like an atom' in the flaming furnace of His own,
He said: 'There, my well-beloved, is a precious
gage of my love piercing your side with a tiny
spark of its brightest flames.'

It was never to be extinguished.

'And as a sign that this great grace is not
imaginary and that it is the foundation of all the
other graces I am still to give you, though I have
closed the wound in your side, the pain of the
wound will remain for ever; and if till now you
have willed to be called only my slave, I give you
the name of the well-beloved disciple of my Sacred
Heart.'

She remained some days 'as though on fire and
intoxicated' with the secret that humility caused
her to keep hidden. But a little after, on a Friday
we may suppose, early in the year 1674 she had a
new vision. The Sacred Heart was shown to her
'enthroned in flames, more dazzling than the sun
and transparent as crystal, bearing that adorable
wound; and it was ringed round with a crown of

thorns signifying the sufferings our sins cause it; and there was a cross over it signifying that from the earliest instant of the Incarnation, that is from the very instant that the Sacred Heart was formed, the Cross was planted in it . . .' And God expressed His desire to be honoured in all places under the figure of his heart of flesh, 'the ultimate effort of His love' as 'a favour to men' and to set them once more 'in these last ages . . . under the sweet liberty of the empire of His love'.

It was in accord with this vision that Margaret Mary made a drawing of the figure which the Church venerates to-day — the flame, the crown of thorns, the Cross.

In the same year 1674, within the octave of Corpus Christi, before the Blessed Sacrament exposed, she received the third message. Our Lord appeared with five suns, His five wounds; and the most brilliant of the five was in His side, the living source of all love. He spoke as in times past of the ingratitude of men and called upon Margaret Mary to make up for all that was wanting. He gave her the means for so great an act of love by a flame so agonizing that she thought she would be 'consumed' in it. She cried out, 'Have pity on my weakness.' 'I shall be your strength,' Our Lord replied.

And He told her what He required of her; first, to receive Him in the Blessed Sacrament; second, always to do so without fail on the first Friday of the month; third, every week on the night of Thursday or Friday, to lie prostrate for an hour, her face to the earth, to share the 'mortal sadness' which He had chosen for His own in the Garden of Olives. These three commands she was to fulfil within the limits of the obedience owed to her superiors.

Margaret Mary could no longer stand, nor utter a word. They raised her from the ground, and brought her before the Superior; to whom she presented herself as a criminal and told her vision.

The contempt she met consoled her and restored her peace. There followed 'a great fever unceasing' with more than sixty fits and agony unbearable. Mère de Saumaise, wishing to test her, ordered her to ask God for a cure as the sure sign that her words were true: if this sign were given the Superior would permit her to follow her Lord's instructions. She yielded to obedience, asked for the miracle and was cured instantly — a formidable trial for her humility, for all eyes were upon her and not all were hostile or contemptuous. But God recalled her to the reality of things by setting before her eyes 'the picture of what she was'. In the light of truth a soul, even a saint's soul, is intolerably ugly. 'What hast thou, oh dust and ashes, wherein thou canst glory?'

There seems to have been a space of nearly a year before the fourth solemn manifestation: it was in 1675, with the reign of Louis XIV at the highest point of its glory; possibly, as before, it was in the octave of Corpus Christi. Before the Blessed Eucharist, Margaret Mary was 'seized with the desire to render love for love' to her Master.

'You can render me no greater love than by doing what I have so many times asked of you.'

Then He showed her plainly His divine Heart and continued: '*Behold this Heart which has so loved men* that it has spared nothing but has been poured out totally and consumed as proof of its love; and for gratitude I receive from the greater part only ingratitude, by their acts of irreverence and sacrilege and by the coldness and the contempt they have for me in this Sacrament of love. But what touches me closest is that the very hearts which are consecrated to me act thus. Because of that I ask of you that the first Friday after the octave of Corpus Christi be dedicated to a special feast to give honour to my Heart, by receiving Communion that day and making reparation for the indignity offered to it during the time it has been exposed on the altar. I promise you that my Heart will expand and spread abundantly the influences of its divine Love upon those who pay it this honour and those who procure that it shall be paid.'

## VI

A PLEASING task for the poor child — to institute or at least cause to be instituted a new feast of the Church! As Bossuet would have said: 'What a work! And what an instrument.' Within her own mind, the Mother Superior was inclined to be for her. She had had her examined by priests, expert in such matters, and they all concluded that it was illusion. But God had just brought to Paray Père de la Colombière, a most holy Jesuit who was willing to share the burden. The vision of their two hearts fused in one within the Sacred Heart sealed their alliance. From now on, there were two camps in the cloister — the sisters who held Margaret Mary for a saint, and those who held her for a lunatic, even perhaps possessed by the devil — they 'threw holy water over her' as they went by her. They were right in thinking that the devil was about, but not where they thought him. How was she to win them over?

Once more — as always — by suffering. God had told her that from now on she must not hope to amass any store of merit for herself. He had closed her personal account. Of all that she was to suffer, far passing all that she had yet suffered, nothing was for her profit but only for others; all was to be poured into the common treasury of love.

To begin with, He revealed to her that His Father, armed in His wrath, was on the point of executing His justice upon the Community of Paray. That the punishment might not fall upon them all, let her offer herself 'His victim for immolation'.

The measure of her suffering was full already: God doubled it. For when she hesitated, God laid it upon her to accept the part of victim no longer as a secret between herself and Him, but publicly.

In the presence of all the sisters she must declare herself chosen by God to make expiation in their stead. The night before she was to make this sacrifice, she tells us, God 'favoured me with a tiny fragment of the sorrowful night of His own Passion'. When the moment came to make the declaration, twenty times she stumbled and fell beneath the cross and cried out that she could carry it no farther. At last, upon the order of her Superior, on her knees and scarcely breathing, she did what God required.

We may imagine the scandal. She — to speak in the name of God; to accuse her sisters; to set herself up as a martyr! But, honour thus satisfied, it seems that the sisters really did look more closely into themselves and see themselves more truly; the convent returned to something like peace.

## VII

She had not yet won. Her passion was not yet over. On her breast she bore the name of her Saviour which she had cut there with a knife; and in her side was that pain which came to agony on each first Friday of the month. They had to bleed her, such was the burning pressure of blood with her. There were still in the convent stout souls who would not accept her; but for all that she found too much honour paid to her, too little to the divine Heart. After a thousand tribulations, she was made mistress of novices. Only then, in 1685, were honours rendered in the novitiate (but still secretly) to the emblem she had drawn with a pen on a sheet of paper; it was the first consecration. But the fire had caught and would not die; it spread steadily; one by one, the nuns yielded. On the twenty-first of June 1686, the first Feast of the

Sacred Heart was officially celebrated in the convent of Paray-le-Monial.

Margaret Mary lived four years more. Why? That she might inform the King of France, 'Eldest son of His Sacred Heart', that the Sacred Heart claims 'to reign in his palace, to be painted on his standard, to be engraved on his arms'; and that it will make him 'triumphant over all the enemies of Holy Church'. Either Louis XIV never received the letter or he refused to reply. But the command still stands. It was on the feast of Saint Louis of France that Margaret Mary had made her profession.

## VIII

She saw that she was dying — though the doctors did not; dying simply of love for God, after a short and mysterious illness. On the seventeenth of October 1690, at the fourth anointing, she gave up her soul to God, pronouncing the name of Jesus Christ, in the arms of two of her novices. 'A whiteness came over her face which was pleasing to be seen.' All the children were crying out in the town: 'Let us go and see the saint who has died at the Saintes-Maries.'

Miracles began at once. But the greatest miracle was that at the small flame of her love — small beside God's if immense beside ours — she should have lighted the torch whose rays now shine over all the earth. The fire took nearly two centuries to catch. She was not beatified until 1864, nor canonized till 1920. Paray is still there as ever, a big village, scarcely a town, with its unpretentious river, the great rough basilica, the small streets of old France and the still numerous convents. One might fancy that the old town had decided to call a halt to its own life when the saint ended hers — that in her it had justified its existence, achieved enough for one town, and had nothing to contribute to or hope from what is called progress. Its silence holds the memory of the girl, behind the high walls never to be passed without reverence and in the chapel where prayer never ceases.

Our thankless age must re-learn at Paray to love the Love of God.